The Nature Kid's Guide to
GUINEA PIGS

DAVID ANDERSON

For information address LP Media Inc. Publishing,
30012 Variolite St NW, Princeton MN 55371
www.lpmedia.org

Publication Data

Guinea Pigs
The Nature Kid's Guide to Guinea Pigs — First edition.

Summary: "Learn all about Guinea Pigs, the Nature Kid Way"
— Provided by publisher.

ISBN: 979-8-89818-238-0

[1. Guinea Pigs – Non-Fiction] I. Title.

Title: The Nature Kid's Guide to Guinea Pigs

CONTENTS

PIGGY PALS

Guinea pigs can learn their own names and will come running when you call them!

Pitter pat! A fluffy guinea pig waddles up to say hello.

Guinea pigs are small, round, and covered in soft fur, with big curious eyes that seem to take in everything around them. They are one of the most popular pets on Earth, and it is easy to see why.

These little animals are naturally social and full of personality. They make a whole range of sounds including squeaks, purrs, and rumbles, each one meaning something different.

Wild guinea pigs originally came from South America, where they lived in groups on grassy open plains. The friendly little pet in your classroom or neighbor's home is descended from those same animals.

WILD ROOTS

FUN FACT!
People in South America kept
guinea pigs over 3,000 years ago —
longer than cats have been pets!

Whoosh! A wild guinea pig zips through the tall grass.

Wild guinea pigs come from South America. Long ago, they lived in grassy hills high in the Andes Mountains. People there began to keep them as pets.

These wild cousins are a bit smaller than pet guinea pigs. They have brown or gray fur to hide in grass, which helps them stay safe from hawks and snakes.

Over time, pet guinea pigs got new coat colors. But they still munch on grass and hay just like their wild relatives. Some things never change!

POCKET PIGS

FUN FACT!
Guinea pigs are not related to pigs at all — they are rodents, like hamsters and mice!

Squish! A chubby guinea pig plops down in its owner's lap.

A guinea pig is small enough to fit right in your hands. Most are about ten inches long from nose to rump. That is a little shorter than a school ruler.

Full grown guinea pigs weigh two to three pounds. Small enough to carry easily, but solid and warm and very much alive in your hands.

Guinea pigs come in many sizes, colors, and coat types. Some are tiny and sleek, others big and fluffy. But every single one is the perfect size for a cozy sit in your lap.

FUZZY FEATURES

DID YOU KNOW?

Guinea pigs have four toes on their front feet but only three on their back feet!

Yawn! A guinea pig opens its mouth and shows its strong teeth.

A guinea pig has a round, pudgy body with short legs and tiny ears. It has almost no tail at all! Big, dark eyes sit on the sides of its head to help it watch for danger.

Look at those teeth! Guinea pigs have teeth that never stop growing. Chewing on hay every day keeps their teeth just the right size.

Each foot has little toes with claws. These help guinea pigs grip the ground when they run and play.

SUPER SNIFFERS

A guinea pig uses its long whiskers to feel its way through tight spaces in the dark!

Sniff sniff! A guinea pig smells a treat from across the room.

Guinea pigs have a powerful sense of smell. They can sniff out food from far away, and a good nose helps them find yummy treats before they even see them.

Small ears help them hear well too. They pick up sounds that people miss, so talk softly so you do not scare them.

Each eye sits on the side of the head. This lets guinea pigs see almost all the way around without turning. They can spot danger from nearly every direction!

COOL COATS

There are over 13 different guinea pig breeds, including the "Skinny pig" that has almost no fur!

Swish! A long-haired guinea pig shows off its silky fur.

Guinea pigs come in many coat types. Some have short, smooth fur. Others have long hair that flows like a tiny wig and needs daily brushing.

There are also curly-haired guinea pigs! Their soft curls feel like wool. Some even have swirls on top of their heads called **rosettes**.

Coats come in white, black, brown, red, and gold. Some guinea pigs have patches of two or three colors mixed together. Every pig is truly one of a kind!

MUNCH TIME
DID YOU KNOW?
Guinea pigs eat some of their own droppings to get extra vitamins — it sounds gross but keeps them healthy!

Crunch! A guinea pig bites into a crispy piece of hay.

Hay is the main food for guinea pigs. They need to munch on it every single day. It keeps their belly happy and their teeth worn down.

Fresh vegetables are important too. Guinea pigs love bell peppers, lettuce, and carrots. Like humans, their bodies cannot make vitamin C on their own, so they need to get it from the food they eat.

Guinea pigs need clean fresh water available at all times. Sweet or salty human foods can make them very sick. The right diet keeps a guinea pig healthy, active, and full of energy.

TRICK TIME

Some guinea pigs learn to push a ball, jump through hoops, and even give high-fives!

Click! A guinea pig spins in a circle for a yummy treat.

Guinea pigs are smart little animals. They can learn tricks when motivated by snacks. A small treat guides them through each new step.

Simple behaviors come first, like coming when called. A guinea pig will connect the sound of its name with a food reward quickly when the treat follows immediately.

Short lessons work best, just five minutes at a time. With patience and consistency, a guinea pig may learn to spin, stand up, or run through a small tunnel.

WHEEK
WHEEK

Wheek! A hungry guinea pig calls out for its dinner.

Guinea pigs talk with many sounds. A loud wheek means they want food or attention. A soft purr means they feel safe and cozy.

Sometimes they chatter their teeth. Watch out! This means they are upset or scared. If you hear it, give them some space.

A rumble is a low, buzzy sound that males make to get attention. Listen closely and you will learn what your pig is trying to tell you!

Guinea pigs make over ten different sounds — more than most other rodent pets!

PLAY HARD

FUN FACT!

A toilet paper roll stuffed with hay makes a free toy that guinea pigs love to toss around!

Rustle! A guinea pig digs into a pile of crinkly paper.

Guinea pigs love to play every day. You can give them tunnels, balls, and paper bags to explore. They enjoy checking out new things.

Try hiding a treat in a paper cup. Your pig will sniff and nudge until it finds the prize. It is a fun game for both of you!

Crinkly paper and small boxes make great toys too. Let your pig push them around and climb inside. Playtime keeps your pet healthy, happy, and never bored.

POP AND ZOOM!

DID YOU KNOW?
A guinea pig can run almost six miles per hour. But they tire out fast!

Pop! A happy guinea pig jumps into the air like a piece of popcorn.

Guinea pigs run fast for their size. They zip around and make sharp turns that will make you smile.

A happy pig may pop straight up in the air! This fun move is called **popcorning**. It looks like a fuzzy little jumping bean bouncing around the cage.

Guinea pigs do not jump or climb much. They stay low to the ground. But those short legs can really zoom when they get excited!

BUSY DAYS

DID YOU KNOW?
Guinea pigs only sleep about four hours total each day, broken into tiny naps!

Munch munch! A pair of guinea pigs start their day with a breakfast of hay!

Guinea pigs are busy little animals. They eat, nap, and play many times each day. They take short naps but never sleep through the whole night like you do.

In the morning, they like to munch and stretch. After eating, they explore and play. Then they rest again before starting over.

Dawn and dusk are when guinea pigs are most active. That is when the squeaking, popcorning, and racing around is most likely to happen. A full hay rack keeps them happily busy through it all.

PIGGY PACKS

FUN FACT!
In Switzerland, it is against the law to own just one guinea pig because they get too lonely!

Squee! Two guinea pigs bump noses and snuggle up side by side.

Guinea pigs are social animals. They do best when they live with a friend. A lone guinea pig can feel sad and bored without company.

Two guinea pigs will play, chat, and snuggle together. They talk to each other all day long and feel safer with a companion nearby. A pair is much more active and entertaining than a single animal living alone.

In the wild, guinea pigs live in groups and are never truly alone. That instinct for company stays strong in pet guinea pigs too, no matter how comfortable their home is.

FINDING LOVE

Rumble! A male guinea pig struts in a circle and wiggles.

When a male guinea pig likes a female, he puts on a show. He walks in circles around her, swaying his body and puffing up his fur to look big.

The female may sniff him back. If she likes him, she will let him stay close. If not, she simply walks away.

Guinea pigs can have babies when they are very young. For this reason, males and females that live together are usually kept in separate cages unless their owners want them to breed.

TINY PUPS

Guinea pig pups are born ready to go — they can eat solid food on their very first day!

Peep! A brand-new guinea pig pup opens its tiny eyes.

Baby guinea pigs are called **pups**. They are born with fur, open eyes, and tiny teeth already in place. They can walk and run within just a few hours!

Most **litters** have two to four pups. Each pup is about the size of your fist. They are so small and cute!

Pups start to nibble on hay and veggies right away. They grow fast and get bigger every day. Soon they will be ready to explore the world on their own.

GROWING UP

Young guinea pigs learn by copying the older pigs around them — monkey see, monkey do!

Thump thump! A growing pup bounces towards its mother.

Mother guinea pigs feed their pups with milk. Pups drink milk for about three weeks while also learning to eat hay.

By three weeks old, pups are ready to be on their own. They can eat, drink, and play without any help. They grow stronger every single day.

At about six months, a guinea pig is almost full grown. Now it can join a new family and bring joy to its new home. A young guinea pig is full of energy and love!

PIGGY POWER

A guinea pig can remember a trick it learned three months ago — that is better than a hamster, which forgets most things in just a few days!

Pop! A guinea pig leaps with joy as it spots its owner.

Guinea pigs have great memories. They can learn paths through mazes and remember where their food bowl is kept for months.

These tiny pets know their owners well. A guinea pig learns your voice and your smell. It can tell you apart from strangers! Pretty smart for such a little pet.

Guinea pigs also have a strong sense of time. They seem to know exactly when meals are coming. That is why they start squeaking right before you feed them!

A guinea pig's cage should be at least 7.5 square feet — any smaller and they won't have enough room to play!

Yip! A happy guinea pig sits in its cage, ready to play.

If you decide to get a pet guinea pig, there are a few things you should know. Good care makes a happy guinea pig. Give your pig a big cage with soft bedding, plenty of hay, fresh water, and a cozy place to hide.

Clean the cage every week. Remove old bedding and wash the water bottle. A clean home keeps your pet healthy and smelling fresh.

Take your guinea pig to the vet once a year for a checkup. Brush its fur and trim its nails regularly. With love and good care, your pig will be happy for years to come!

GLOSSARY

rodent
A type of animal with front teeth that never stop growing.

rosette
A swirl of fur on a guinea pig's head or body.

popcorning
A happy jump that guinea pigs do when excited.

litter
A group of baby animals born at the same time.

pup
A baby guinea pig.